Botched

But

Beautiful

Beulah Neveu

BeNeveu Words, Inc.

Publishing Company

Rosenberg, Texas

Botched But Beautiful

BeNEVEU WORDS, INC.

Publishing Company
BeNeveu Words, Inc. Publishing Company
Rosenberg, TX 77471

Copyright © 2015 Beulah Neveu

ISBN-13 DIGIT: 978-0-692-52365-0
ISBN-10 DIGIT: 0692523650
Library of Congress Control Number: 2015914394
Manufactured in the United States of America

First Edition

Also Available
From Beulah Neveu

Bracie

Bracie is a Christian love story about faith, family, and friends. It tells the story of a quest for true love and the uncertainty of the very thing that is being searched for. It's a story about the strength and unity of family in the good times and the not so good.

A Cry For Home

The journey of six people as they discover, money can buy you a house, but only God can make it a HOME.

Visit beneveuwords4you.com for more information about Bracie, A Cry For Home and upcoming titles from Beulah Neveu.

Acknowledgements

First, I would like to thank God for blessing me with the gift of writing. I am so grateful that He has allowed me to see one of the dreams of my youth come true, being able to share my poetry. I thank Him for bringing me through the dark days so not only would I be able to see His light, but to appreciate it. I thank my Heavenly Father for using every season of my life as an opportunity for my good and His glory.

I would like to thank my husband Thomas Jr. for being my inspiration and strength. I thank him for being my spiritual cover and for loving and encouraging me on my journey of healing. I thank him for his prayers and support in my every endeavor. Mostly, I would like to thank him for teaching me how to let the words buried in my heart flow freely.

I would like to thank my mother Verna LaCour for being my greatest example of living a godly life. I would like to thank her for teaching me, with God all things really are possible and He will never put more on me than I can bear. I would like to thank my children Verna2, DeAnthany Sr., DeJuan Sr., and DeRaymond Sr. for their love, encouragement, and support. I thank them for all the times they made me laugh, gave me proud mama moments, and mostly, for always believing in me.

I would like to acknowledge my daughters in law Romesha, Tiffany, and Tina for loving my sons and encouraging me.

I would like to thank my wonderful grandchildren for their love and support. You are part of the reason I do what I do.

I would also like to acknowledge a few people who have pushed me into all that God has for me. They are listed in no particular order: The ladies of Woman2Woman, my sisters Myranda Davis and Lolita Woods and her husband Curtis, my brothers Donald and Albert Hall, Keith T. Walker, Doug and Ronda James, Joyce Toussant, Isabell Pitts, Pastors Eric and Phyllis Wiggins, and my pastors, Pastor Gusta Booker, Jr. and Pastor Ronald Booker, Sr.

BOTCHED BUT BEAUTIFUL

I would like to thank Jennifer Lee for critiquing my poetry, my dream.

I would like to give special acknowledgement and thanks to my late brother Herman Hall Jr. who never allowed me to give up on my dream of one day publishing my poetry. I am and will always be his BZ.

I would like to thank everyone who has supported me, encouraged me, and who has prayed for me.

Be Blessed and Enjoy!

Rusty's Poem

She's very pretty and very small

Her loving smile shows it all.

Her hair is long, her face is round,

Her eyes are soft and pretty brown.

She is never still, she is on the run.

She is always game for having fun.

She's not very old, she is only three.

She is my little girl, her name is Rusty.

(My first poem written September 25, 1981)

From A Little Child

Lord up above, I'm just a child.

Please let me talk to You, for just a little while.

I can't use a lot of words, for I'm still young in age,

BOTCHED BUT BEAUTIFUL

I'm learning to understand Your ways as I
turn my Bible pages.

I have learned that You love me from the
depths of Your heart.

There is nothing or no one that can make Your
love part.

I know that You gave me the right to the tree
of life

And all that You require of me is the way that
is right.

Right now I want to say, "Thank you." All
though You're busy as can be,

You've taken a little time to listen to me.

(Written from Verna's prayer at the age of five
years old)

My Son

I remember when you were a baby, totally
dependent on me.

Around the age of five I had to set you free.

I watched as you grew older and learn to speak your mind.

You never gave me any trouble, well, at least most of the time.

You are a young man now, and you walk the path.

You have chosen to live whole and avoid God's eternal wrath.

Soon you will reach manhood, and the race you'll continue to run.

Always remember, no matter where you go in life

You will always be my son.

My Son (2)

He's my son standing strong and tall

With pride and courage,

God gives him strength to conquer all.

He is my son so brilliant and true,

BOTCHED BUT BEAUTIFUL

With the fear of the Lord guiding him
through.

He is my son from a prayer that I prayed.

I watch him with pride as he walks by faith.

He is my son from God's great treasure.

His love is abundant, it has no measure.

So, with honor and respect, and all that is due,

He is my son, but Lord I give him back to You.

Enough Love

Sometimes I know you wonder if I love you all
the same,

Because you are as different as the meaning of
your names.

Never doubt that I have enough love for you,

You all are gifts from God above.

I thank Him by teaching you to stand on His
Holy Word.

I love you all with a sincerity that can come from no other,

With warmth and protection can only come from your mother.

Because I Love You

From the first time I saw you, which was the day that you were born,

I knew you were special when they laid you in my arms.

We have laughed through the years when we played with your dolls and dishes.

We jumped and we cheered when you got your birthday wishes.

Now I watch as you achieve one goal after another.

Your make me very proud to say that I am your mother.

You are a young lady now and your innocent smile I can still see.

BOTCHED BUT BEAUTIFUL

You will always be "Mama's Baby." No one
can take that away from me.

This poem was written for no special occasion.
I tell you this because it's true.

You are a very special daughter and I will
always love you.

How You Came To Be

One day my daughter asked me, "Mama, how
did I come to be?"

I smiled and said to her, "Baby, God gave you
especially to me.

God took the clay of love and mold it into a
little girl.

He placed her in my body until she was ready
for the world.

God gave me the strength to carry you the
whole time through.

He blessed me with wisdom so I would know
what to do.

He touched me September 20th, very late that night."

 He said, "Mama it is time for your daughter to see the light."

"I pushed and I helped as much as I was able, the hours

Passed quickly, then I saw you on the table.

Early the next morning I waited anxiously,

For them to bring me my daughter who had just come to be."

For the Youth

Your youthfulness is great, but it does not last long,

Don't take it for granted for soon it will be gone.

Each morning you rise, give thanks for another day,

Hold to God's unchanging hand, walk with Him, and pray.

BOTCHED BUT BEAUTIFUL

Being a youth is not for parties, drinking, and living wild.

Your body is still a temple that God must dwell inside.

Use this time as a testimony, that God can use the young, too.

So, no matter what your peers think, you'll know God will see you through.

Take this message seriously, think about the things you have done.

Will the Lord be able to say to you, "Servant well done?"

My Mother

He voice is soft, her heart is wide,

Her arms are open to take you inside.

She always smiles, she is never down,

On her face is never a frown.

Whenever she is needed, she is always there

To help you out and to offer you prayer.

She is always happy, she is filled with love.

It is given to her by the Lord above.

She is one of a kind, there is no other.

She is my special love, she is my mother.

The Love of Family

We started out as children and though the years we have grown.

Now, God has blessed us with children of our own.

Now we sit and watch some of the funny things they do.

We look and we laugh because we did them, too.

We see ourselves in our children. I can see you in mine, too.

So, many of their capers certainly are not new.

BOTCHED BUT BEAUTIFUL

Now that we're all grown up and we think about the past,

We share our special times of memories that will last.

Our childhood was happy when we were all together.

We were strengthened through the years by

Life's different kinds of weather.

Each year the LORD blesses us with His presence from above,

We must never forget how sisters and brothers fill the home with love.

Fathers

When God made man and said it is good,

He expected fathers to live like real men should.

He gave fathers courage and the ability to be strong.

He gave them wisdom not to lead his children
wrong.

He meant for fathers to be examples of men
taking a Christian stand,

To let his sons know the world has a demand
for a real man.

So men, when you want to know what true
fathering should be,

Get your Bible, open it up, and focus on
Calvary.

Happy Birthday

Another birthday has come and we celebrate
with cheer,

For we know it was the Lord who brought you
through the year.

He touched you every day with His love and
His grace.

He blessed you with strength to continue your
Christian race.

17

The past year has made you stronger than you've ever been before.

Hold on, stand firm, God is going to bless you even more.

Happy Birthday Daughter

I see a young lady now that was mama's little girl,

With lacy ruffle socks, ponytails, and curls.

You've grown through the years and you are beautiful as can be.

You are a precious young lady, very courteous and sweet.

I watch you take on responsibilities that seem kind of hard.

I see you work them through with the help of the Lord.

As you go through another year may each day be blessed,

As God fills it, with love and happiness.

My Assignment

I sat humbled, but still very confused.

"What is it?" I asked God, "that You want me to do?"

I could hear Him clearly, "You are my vessel and I am ready to use you."

I picked up the pen and paper I had sitting on the table.

"I'm ready Lord, I'm willing, and with Your Holy Spirit guiding me

I know that I am able."

Every night I kept to my assignment. Hour after hour I would write.

Never checking or reading back, I only used His guidance as my light.

Two months and one week later, I held in my hand what God had given me.

Once again I could hear Him clearly, "Your assignment will be titled Bracie."

I wanted to dive into Bracie's story, but God assured me, it wasn't time.

19

BOTCHED BUT BEAUTIFUL

He didn't want me to change anything, for Bracie's life I would soon find out was really partly mine.

Bracie's debut had come and gone and its story was drawing attention

To areas in my life, to my family I had never mentioned.

I was shocked, yet pleasantly surprised by the many comments and reviews.

The transparency everyone was talking about was coming to me as news.

By God's instructions I finally read Bracie's story.

I sat stunned, I was paralyzed by the fear that gripped me.

For a moment I was upset with God. Yes, like you would not believe.

"Why Father, would You allow people to see so deep within me?"

"WHY ME, LORD?" I finally got the courage to ask.

His answer, "I have been calling you for service for quite a while.

Because you were ashamed of hurts being revealed,

You kept running and trying to hide."

God told me, "Beulah, I healed you a long time ago.

What I really need you to see is, now you have been made whole."

At First I didn't understand the depths of Bracie's story.

God had used me to show His healing, faithfulness, and love.

Because He removed my hands, now He would get the glory.

So many people commented on a dream that was not mine.

I'm not ungrateful, yet I must tell the truth.

Bracie is not a dream come true. It is an assignment

God had especially for me to do.

BOTCHED BUT BEAUTIFUL

The Letter

I rushed in from work and there was your
letter.

I picked it up and smiled, I still cannot explain
the feeling that I felt.

I knew my life was about to change, it would
be for better.

I held on to it, for what seems like forever.

Even before I read the first line

I knew this letter would carry me to the end of
my time.

I saw we both had been praying, asking God
for that special someone.

We both knew right away our searching now
was done.

After all these years I still read that first letter.

The words are engraved in my heart. It was in
that letter you declared,

God sent you an angel and brought your soul
out of the dark.

Precious Love

It's from the depths of our love that my heart
has new life.

When I close my eyes you are there,

When I think about how much God loves me,
you are there.

When it seems I can't go on and want to give
up,

The Holy Spirit comforts my soul.

He simply says, "Someone is praying for you."

That alone gives me strength to push on.

I pray the world will be able to see

The blessed love that God has given us.

Mostly I pray they will see the precious hand

Of our kind, loving, forgiving, and faithful
God.

You Touch My Soul

Your love is important to my life,

Worth more than silver or gold.

You have reached through my heart

And touched the depths of my soul.

I'm Not Her

How many times must I tell you, I'm not her,
I'm not them.

I'm not deceiving in my words.

I say what I mean and I mean what I say.

There is no need to read between the lines,

The truth is not deferred.

I speak my message loud and clear,

I'm not her.

With me there's no need to look over your
shoulder or wonder what kind of drama is
next.

I have no game or ulterior motives.

I give you my all, I give you my best.

You are safe now, for I cherish you with all my heart.

Soon all of the past will be just a blur

When you learn and trust the fact that

I'm not her.

Cheating? Please!

I sit here wondering what just happened. Why are you so angry?

Don't you know by now you are not my first or second choice?

Listen to me, hear my voice, you my dear are my only choice.

I cannot share what is not mine to give.

My body is my temple, it is holy, and it is pure.

It is set aside for your pleasure, of this I am sure.

BOTCHED BUT BEAUTIFUL

So settle down and enhance your calm,

I will never be found in another man's arms.

I cannot, I will not mistreat what we have
been given.

Baby, it is for God and for you that I am living.

Don't let the enemy whisper evil thoughts in
your ear.

 Know God's strength is made perfect in your
weakness

And His peace is always near.

Trust God, in who He has called me to be.

Cheater and liar will never be associated with
me.

I stand firm in who I am, I am yours.

I am a one man's woman.

What's In A Kiss?

What's in a kiss that is filled with desire?

A touch, a feeling, a heart burning with fire?

What's in a kiss that makes me tremble inside?

A kiss that makes my body burn with a longing I cannot hide.

What's in a kiss that makes me keep wanting more?

A kiss that makes me feel like I'm gliding on a soothing ocean shore.

What's in a kiss when you are holding me close to you?

Your hold is tight and secure. Your hold is daring and true.

What's in a kiss when your lips are touching mine?

It's the warmth and wholeness, a kiss that's truly mine.

Just For You

If I could have the sky to place in my hand,

I would give it all to my one special man.

If I could have the sand from the desert or beach,

I wouldn't be able to count the ways of heights our love could reach.

If I could have the stars that hang out in space,

I would put them in my dreams so I could see your face.

If I could have the sun with its rays so bright,

Surely I could have the moon to take us through the night.

The Awesome Beauty of Love

Let him kiss me with the kisses of his mouth: for thy love is better than wine.

Song of Solomon 1:2

BOTCHED BUT BEAUTIFUL

Day 1

God's voice demands attention, its power so
great the elements had to take form. Yet we
hear His voice so lovingly and we choose to
stand still in defiance. We think we know
what is best for our fragile lives when we don't
even control if we will breathe from one
moment to the next.

 My husband, my lover, my friend, I'm sitting
in the window of this great ship looking out on
an even greater awareness of God's great
power. Water so beautiful it looks as if God's
hand stirred the perfect shades of blue and
poured it out to create such a splendor. Water
so perfect because God had only to speak and
it became so, with no help from man or
angels.

I sit here thinking about how much Almighty
God loves me. He has allowed me to see so
much of His creation so that my eyes can be
openly aware of who He truly is. For so long I
was not aware of God's power or His love for
me. The enemy had distorted my vision. He
distorted my image of me at the tender age of
5 years old. That was the first of several times

I had been touched inappropriately by someone I trusted. The enemy distorted my image of love and watched as my path took a destructive turn from the innocent little girl I was created to be.

I have been on cruises before and I have also sat at windows like this before. Today is different. Today I am being empowered by the Word of God. Today, I truly understand, He never turned His head from me, but from the sinful act. He did not toss me out or to the side. He knew then, that same distorted act would help shape me into the woman of God that I am today. He knew that my distorted view of love would change to glorify Him with a sincere godly love. I went through pain and adversity to now know that God is faithful.

As I sit here looking at what God spoke into existence I know there really is NOTHING too hard for Him. I understand He has had it all in his control from the very beginning. The beauty of God's spoken Word cannot be described with our finite vocabulary. If we could somehow describe it with one word, maybe it would be awesome or maybe even glorious. Today, I will use LOVE. It is the

BOTCHED BUT BEAUTIFUL

foundation of all God does. As I see the perfection of this blue water, I see the perfection of God's love for me. He not only kept me, he cleaned me up. He took me from nothingness to being a usable vessel for Him. He took the distorted lies and molded me into a servant, a child, a member of the royal priesthood.

God knew I would not be strong enough to do this on my own so He brought me to you. I wish so much that I could say I love you with a perfect love, but that is not possible. I know the only love that is perfect is the love God has given us through His son Jesus Christ. So it is out of that perfection that I Love You! God's love for us is like His sunshine, full of warmth and goodness. I believe no one can improve on what God has given us or done for us. We must make a conscience decision to bask in the glorious love He has so freely given us. Today, with each breath God allows me to breathe I honor him in how I love you. It's with sincerity, honesty, and purity that I give you my all, I give you me!

Day 2

Beautiful blue skies and water as far as the eyes can see. So is God's awesomeness for us. We were two souls seeking true love, but only found hurt, pain, deceit, and betrayal. God's Word says we will suffer persecution for His sake. At that time in our lives we did not know or understand our suffering was allowed by Him, so in the end it would be used for Him. God has taught me suffering is but for a while, in its course we should learn to praise, honor, and glorify Him, 1 Peter: 6-7.

God also promises as we overcome suffering we will be perfected, established, strengthened, and settled in Him, 1 Peter 5:10. Our love and marriage is centered in Christ and established and strengthened on a solid foundation in Him. Because of that we are now being perfected, day by day, to live for Him in happiness greater than either of us has ever known.

As I look out of this window I understand God's loving provision has no end. His love will continue on even when we no longer exist.

BOTCHED BUT BEAUTIFUL

God's love for us is limitless. He is calling us to trust Him completely. He sees the unfair persecution we have endured, but He has made us free in Him. Even in suffering God has given us favor. He knew in His realm of favor you would need a help meet. He trained me to be a wife who would be holy and acceptable to Him first. He taught me submission and what it really means to honor my husband in the LORD. He knew I was ready when I called out to Him from my heart. He looked into my heart, while looking into yours and He answered our prayers.

My husband we have endured for such a time as this. The same almighty God who spoke this beautiful water into being is the same God that spoke to my heart and said "You don't understand my plan, just trust Me." It is the same soft and loving voice that has told me in my time of prayer that, "Everything is going to be all right." I trust His voice. I now understand its power. I understand it does not lie. He only requires that I believe and trust in His perfect timing.

I sit and gaze on one form of God's awesome perfection, perfectly blue, perfectly powerful, and perfectly set in place. As I look over this great ocean I know there is nothing man can do to alter God's perfect creation. So I pray it will forever be with us as we live in the will of God according to Matthew 19:5-6. We are one in the name of the Father, and of the Son, and the Holy Spirit. No man shall separate us! May our love honor God and embrace His never ending blessings for us and through us. May the persecution we have endured and over come through Him and for Him be a constant reminder of His faithfulness. I pray it will forever remind us to never take what He has so richly given us for granted. I Love you with all that I am and ever hope to be. Be Blessed my Husband!!

Day 3

And God said "Let there be a firmament in the midst of the water," and land came forth.

Adam declared, "She is bone of my bone, flesh of my flesh, she shall be called WOMAN!"

BOTCHED BUT BEAUTIFUL

God's order has stood from the beginning of time. As He spoke He declared "It Is Good!" So is His declaration of LOVE.

Love is the most sought after feeling and/or emotion in the world. When we stop to think about how awesome God is, we would be wise to seek love in Him FIRST! As the land stands out from the sea, so stands God's love for us. It shall not be moved.

Storms have come fierce and determined to destroy, but what God commands to stand will stand. So it is with the love He has commanded of us. We are to be His example of true godly love. The storms of life have come, its forces have been fierce. But, what God has ordained to stand He has empowered with strength to endure.

I sit here looking at how God molded the land as He spoke it from the waters. He moved not His hands. HIS WORD WAS ALL THAT WAS NEEDED!

God has commanded that we love each other as one. He has touched us with his strength to be able to stand. God ask that man cover his bride as He covers His creation. In honoring

God I submit to your headship while I walk beside you as your equal in Him.

I am your good thing

I am bone of your bone

I am flesh of your flesh

I am your WOMAN!

Like the firmament rose to stand at the voice of God, so I rise up to His call to be strong and stable as your wife, your soul mate, and your friend.

As God waters the earth so it is that He pours the essence of his love for you over and into me. For as long as the earth rest on the foundation of God's call, so will I rest in the strength and confidence He has given me through your love.

Day 4

What a beautiful day! I see God's awesome love pouring out through nature. The Bible declares, surely as you have seen nature you have seen the hand of God. The air is so pure

BOTCHED BUT BEAUTIFUL

and clean I find myself taking deep breaths of its freshness.

I look at how beautiful the plants and trees are here. Ninety-eight percent of them are untouched by man's hands, yet they continue to grow in perfect order and perfect color, each growing and blooming in its own created order. Here, in the Cayman Islands, plants grow as large as trees. They seem to stand as royalty in their beauty!

So our lives should be before GOD! We stand as royalty! Our love and marriage is growing in ministry and in its spiritual beauty so that it may strengthen those around us according to God's creative order.

Being your wife and soul mate is like taking a breath of God's fresh air. As I study Philippians 4:8 my mind focuses in on our marriage. I think about the pureness of our hearts as we turn to God in gratitude. God has given us a love that is founded on the truth of His Word through Jesus Christ. I take time to think on these things daily. We have a love, a marriage, and a ministry that lifts God in praise. I stand tall this beautiful morning, in spiritual royalty as I declare boldly,

I am a child and servant of GOD

I am blessed

I am yours!

Day 5

Our stop in Cozumel, Mexico met me with an array of bright and beautiful colors. In the midst of such beauty God once again allowed me to see how awesome He is.

Flowers so vibrant in color they seem to shout out God's glorious power. Yet we have a voice and remain quiet about God's wonderful touch in and on our lives.

I want to share the awesome wonder of God's love for me, for you, for us! I feel like the flowers in Mexico, I want to tell of God's glorious power. I realize more each day how much of God's love is on display in nature around us. It fills us with vibrant color and lavish scents from God's garden of love. A garden that goes with me everywhere I go.

BOTCHED BUT BEAUTIFUL

I understand now why I love roses so much. Their colors are many, yet their scent never changes, so it is with God's love. He allows us to take many paths, but there is only one ultimate destination- To Him!

To get to the true beauty of the rose we must first get past the thorns. We may get stuck several times, but the beauty that is before us gives us the courage to press on. Once we have the rose in our hand and we can smell its melodious scent we know it was worth fighting through.

I have been pricked by the thorns of life, but each time I step into your embrace I know it was worth the fight to behold the beauty of your love. Our love has been touched and ordained by the hands of our Heavenly Father.

I stand as your angel, your flower, and shout out from the awesomeness of God's love: I LOVE YOU!

Day 6

I sit at the window watching the beautiful water as we travel towards home, water so versatile in its perfection. It is fragile enough to glide through our fingers, humble enough to allow us to enjoy its coolness to quench our thirst. Yet it is strong enough to allow us to sail upon her for our pleasure.

God has blessed us to share a love as versatile as the water. A love fragile enough to be treated as a rare jewel, that humbles itself in gratitude, and strong enough to sustain us during times of hardship.

Your love has been my greatest inspiration in finding me. In loving you I have found my true identity. It's in loving you that I have learned to be strong while embracing my femininity. My source and strength in acquiring and understanding true love has been in knowing GOD makes no mistakes. What He has given us was by no chance a mistake or haphazard coincidence. It is a divine plan, for a divine love, by a Divine God.

 I love you. Sometimes it feels like those three words don't seem to be enough to express how

BOTCHED BUT BEAUTIFUL

I truly feel. Then I realize it's how God describes His love for us. So today I pray to the True and Living God who has known and established love at its greatest.

Heavenly Father, I pray asking that the love you have for my husband, you will pour it into me. Allow me to be your essence of love for him. Teach me to understand his ups and downs. Help me to comfort his innermost fears and insecurities. Teach me to love him from my soul and let it be done in humble gratitude. Father, bless our marriage to continue to grow in love and in ministry. May You forever keep us covered with Your love, mercy, and grace, Amen.

Love Is Like

Like the wings of an eagle

That soars in the sky.

Like the stillness of a spring

In the sweet by and by.

Like the song of a canary

So soft and so sweet.

Like the feel of a baby

So tender and so meek.

Like the protection of a bear

Of her young playing cub.

Like the tenderness of a mother

Giving her child a hug.

Like the excitement of a champion

Who has just won first place.

BOTCHED BUT BEAUTIFUL

Like the innocence of a child

With a smile on his face.

Like the trusting and surrendering

Of a pure white dove

Like the beating of my heart

Shall you have the depths of my love.

Committed

We'll follow when you choose to stand and
lead,

 Love us whole heartily and we'll surrender to
your need.

When you're committed and never willing to
quit,

We'll commit with you and willingly submit.

We are the weaker vessel, God said this to be
true,

But you must recognize in our weakness we
are strong, too.

God has equipped us with strength that most can't imagine.

Loosing is never an option, we've been instilled with the instinct to win.

So, when life beats you down and knocks you off track,

Trust us, hear us, know we've always got your back.

We'll stand by you and fight with you,

As long as your cause is meaningful and true.

God made you the man in His own image, right on the spot,

But when He made woman, He was really showing off.

Ok, the kidding aside. When God made woman He knew His creation

Was good,

He made us a help meet, a nurturer, a lover, a wife,

One who would be committed to you for life.

Woman was fashioned around your rib,

So we can walk beside you and encourage you to live.

Show us how much you care, by

Loving us, protecting us, and covering us in prayer.

Becoming One

It is time for me to part from my father and mother,

As I start my life to cleave with another.

The one person I can love from the depths of my heart,

To share my world until death do us part.

The one to share my dreams, my hopes, and my sorrows.

The one who will let me know there is always a better tomorrow.

God set me on this course as I prepare to say "I do." I thank Him sincerely as I anticipate becoming one with you.

Forgive Me

I don't like for us to quarrel, it is frustrating as can be.

Can't you see I'm hurting because you're not talking to me.

I want this spat to be over, just tell me what I must do

To get this quarrel over with, so I can talk with you.

My heart is very empty and I'm feeling really lonely.

Only you can right this wrong that's going on inside of me.

I'm very sorry for my part in making this come about.

I need your forgiveness if we're going to work this out.

Don't punish me forever, please help me to be whole again.

Only you can make this happen by bringing this spat to an end.

No Secrets Before The Father

We can't tip around the presence of God,

For He neither slumbers or sleep.

He is forever watching over us, his dear little sheep."

We need to lay ourselves before the Father

And let God truly heal

The hurt and the pain we've been too ashamed to reveal.

We must lay aside our garments

And strip for God in prayer.

He doesn't use modern medicine,

Only His blood is applied with care.

We must learn to let go

Of things lost in time.

And let God perform healing,

In our souls and on our minds.

We truly don't have long.

Living this life is not a game.

We must surrender to the Father,

Spiritually naked and not ashamed.

A Word Of Encouragement

Things will at times seem to go wrong.

Never doubt the Lord, He won't let it last too long.

Someway, somehow, when you at least expect to find,

God will send someone to give you peace of mind.

Do not hold your head down, unless you do it to pray.

You must know God is listening and He will make away.

When you are feeling down and at the end of your rope,

Hold on, God is there. He will give you hope.

I bring this word of encouragement

To be a blessing for your heart.

Hold it there, keep it safe, and never let it part.

Crosses

What is your idea of a heavy cross to bear?

Not knowing what dress to put on or what suit to wear?

Is your cross a child who refuses to obey,

Or a spouse that is lost and can't find his way?

Is your cross a loved one who would rather be left alone

To fight this cruel world than come to God's blessed home?

Is your cross just living and trying to do your best?

Well, this is a part of life, your cross is just your test.

Now think about the cross that Jesus had to bear.

He had to suffer alone as His Father watched with care.

Jesus had to hang on His cross. He had to give up the ghost,

So we could have a right to live with our heavenly Host.

God's Servant

I may be knocked down,

But I am not broken.

I may not understand,

But I am not stupid.

I may be pushed back,

But I am not forgotten.

I may be hurt,

But I will not be destroyed.

I may be lied upon,

BOTCHED BUT BEAUTIFUL

But I will walk in the truth.

God has brought me with a price.

I am His, because He gave me life.

(Inspired by: 2 Corinthians 4:7-10)

My Destiny

This is my life, the decision is mine,

To throw it away or put my mark in time.

My dream belongs to me, it is my destiny.

It's not your decision to make the choice is
totally up to me.

I have a desire to succeed and I choose not to
wait.

I have a goal to fulfill before it is too late.

Do I sit around and wait for you to validate
me?

Oh, I think not! I must be the woman

God has created me to be.

So don't stand around to see if I'm going to fail.

I'm on the move now, my ship has set sail.

Well Done

A servant came forward as quietly as can be.

She said, "Here is my ticket, the angel gave it to me."

The King took her ticket and looked up her name with care.

"Your name is in the book," He said, "Take your place over there."

She stood before the Master as the Savior sat by His side.

Then she bowed before them as tears flowed from her eyes.

"Glory to the Father, Hallelujah to His Son.

I've made it to heaven and

The victory for me has been won!"

Quiet Time

I like to be alone to get away from the daily grind.

I sit and talk with the Lord, this is my quiet time.

I allow no one to disturb me or put other thoughts in my mind,

No one to call my name, during my quiet time.

When my day seems hectic and peace I cannot find.

I push everything aside and have some quiet time.

A Word of Thanks

For all that you've done, and all that you've shared,

For your love and support and showing you always cared.

For all that you give and the nice things you do,

This word of thanks is just for you.

With each day that passes, may the Lord truly bless,

And fill your days with happiness.

Thank You

How do I say thank you for being there for me?

While I smiled on the outside, inside the tears flowed free.

How do I say thank you for each encouraging word?

Although I showed no emotions, every word was heard.

How do I say thank you, when I thought each day would be my last?

You were there for me to lean on until the troubled days were past.

I can only say thank you by lifting your name in prayer.

If in time you should need me, I promise to be right there.

True Friendship

True friendship is not easily attained and is very seldom kept,

For to have a true friend, you must first be a true friend yourself.

True friends keep a confidence no matter what obstacles appear.

They are faithful in giving godly advice whether they are far or near.

True friends say the right things, at the right time, in the right way.

They take your loyalty seriously as they walk
with you and pray.

 True friendship is based on honesty and
cultivated with love.

To have one true friend is a blessing from the
LORD above.

Hello

I pray you are doing well today.

No matter what happened last night,

Or even this morning, right now

Can be the beginning of a brand new light.

I want to remind you that life has a way of
throwing us a curve,

But don't let it stress you out or get on your
nerves.

Today when someone push your so called
buttons, don't shoot off at the mouth.

BOTCHED BUT BEAUTIFUL

Take a moment and look a little deeper, they may need what only you can give.

A smile, an encouraging word, a reason to let loose, and live.

Today you have been given blessings fresh and new.

I am writing this letter to let you know that I am praying for you.

The Invisible Chair

The Lord told me to hold on,

Don't give up or be in despair.

I am holding you up,

I am your invisible chair.

Walk boldly in My Word, know that I care.

You may stumble, but you won't fall.

I'll catch you, I am your invisible chair.

Walk boldly in my Word, stand alone if you dare.

Don't worry, you are protected,

I am your invisible chair.

The righteous rejoice, but sinners beware.

You have not claimed a right

To Me, the invisible chair.

Pay Attention

Don't turn from God's abundant treasure,

Or you will dwindle away and eat with the swine.

You will surely lose your mind.

Please don't refuse God's offer to come home.

You don't want to live in this cold world abandoned and alone.

I beg of you, don't try to wait until tomorrow

59

BOTCHED BUT BEAUTIFUL

Your soul may end in pain and sorrow.

Wait, don't turn away from God's saving grace
Or hell will be your final resting place.

God is giving you time to say,
"I'm sorry," to repent and pray.

So stop and turn completely around,
Let God place your feet on solid ground.

Take this time and surrender to His love,
And secure your home in Heaven above.

The God I Serve

I can't serve a god that I can hold in my hand.

I can't serve a god the size of mere man.

I can't serve a god whose love is no greater than mine.

I can't serve a god who can't see pass one day at a time.

I can't serve a god who can't pick me up when I am down.

I surely can't serve a god when needed he cannot be found.

I can only serve my Lord, who is Holy and true.

He will never leave me stranded, He will bring me through.

I serve the living Savior who formed the heavens and the earth.

He had my life molded, even before my birth.

I serve Almighty God, who sits high and looks low.

BOTCHED BUT BEAUTIFUL

He washed my dirty heart with red blood

And made it whiter than snow.

The Father's Love

I must tell the news to all of the world,

The heavenly Father loves His little girls.

If you should have a need that seems out of touch,

God can deliver, for He loves His daughters very much.

The Father wants to heal you but He gives you the right to choose.

He's waiting with open arms, with blessings just for you.

No matter what is in your past, whether its heartache or shame.

When God touches your life you will never be the same.

Talith Cumi, means damsel arise, walk into God's great light.

You are a daughter of the Father. You are His joy, His jewel, His delight.

Free To Be Me

I am here now,

I am free to be me.

I look forward to

Walking in my destiny.

I stand humbly, but with courage.

I allow my beauty to shine free,

I am determined to walk in total victory.

I let my words come alive, I speak my mind.

I persevered, I overcame, my sight has been restored,

I am no longer spiritually blind.

I have been ordained to stand,

And empowered to endure,

My feet are planted and my faith is sure.

God is my Father. In Him I found my true identity,

Therefore, I refuse to cower under your scrutiny.

I stand boldly with grace and security,

I declare I am free, yes free to be me.

A Designer's Original

I am a designer's original, a masterpiece of the Master;

Created of flesh and blood, not stone, wood, or plaster.

He created only one like me, I am like no other.

I am a combination of genes from my father and my mother.

On the outside we my look similar, but the inside is where it counts.

My strengths and weaknesses are balanced in Christ where it counts.

To the Master I owe my all, for without Him I would not be.

I thank Him for the opportunity to be His masterpiece.

Don't Judge Me

Don't judge me by the clothes that I wear,

My size, my race, nor the color of my hair.

Don't judge me by the way that I talk.

I may limp or sway, so don't judge me

By the way that I walk.

Don't judge me by the things that I do.

We may not agree on the same issues, so

Don't judge me if I don't think like you.

If you must judge me,

BOTCHED BUT BEAUTIFUL

Judge me on things that are true,

Like my faith in God and

My walk of holiness, too.

I know God will be my final judge.

Only He can see my heart.

He knows the heart of the matter,

Is really a matter of the heart.

I Am A Woman

I am a woman, a creation made.

Adam's rib was the first price paid.

I am a woman standing by my man's side, not behind.

I have intelligence, I have knowledge, I have a mind.

I am a woman created in God's image, too.

I am strong, but soft, yet beautiful, too.

I am a woman. It is through my body new life flows.

It is a gift from God as each generation grows.

So never look down or turn your nose up at me.

BOTCHED BUT BEAUTIFUL

I am a true woman. I am the woman God
created me to be.

Strength and Honor are her clothing.

She opens her mouth with wisdom

and in her tongue is the law of kindness.

Proverbs 31:26

Dedicated to the ladies who

Saw the potential for greatness

Hidden within me, before I could

See it in myself.

BOTCHED BUT BEAUTIFUL

My Mother: Verna D. Hall Lacour

You were my role model even before I knew what it meant to have one.

You loved me with such intensity, before I knew what love was and the lasting effects it has on one's life.

You knew from the day I was born God had given me the potential for greatness.

You must have seen a certain kind of beauty in my little eyes for you chose to give me the name of one of the persons you loved most in this world, your beloved sister Beulah, (It took me a while to learn how beautiful and special she was, but thank God I did.)

Your nurturing spirit has been ongoing all of my life. It took me years to understand the calling God had placed upon you. It was in reading Matthew 25:31-40 that I realized you were always about the Father's business.

I learned at an early age to watch how people live and not always go by the words they spoke. It was in watching you that I learned compassion. I learned to give without expecting anything in return. I learned how to not hold grudges and to turn the offense over to God. You never talked much, but you taught me how to love with sincerity. Today, I realize in watching you live a godly life I can say, "The greatest lesson you taught me was the strength to forgive." As one of your children I lived through some of the abuse that was afflicted upon you, but I'll never know the true extent of it all.

Even in the midst of all the wrong and hard times life dished out, you never lost your smile or your ability to love from the heart. When you had to protect us with your life, you never seemed to regret it.

Seeing you shed tears that dreary, but freeing Saturday morning still touches my heart to this day. I know I was only a child, but it's an image of love and compassion I'll never forget.

I've told you through the years that I love you. I pray that as you and the world read this, you will know I not only love you, I respect you, and I honor you. I have, I am, and I'll always thank our Heavenly Father for choosing you Verna Dean Davis Hall LaCour to be my mother, my true example of the virtuous woman of Proverbs 31:10-31.

BOTCHED BUT BEAUTIFUL

My Mentor: Dr. Theola Booker

You took me under your wings at the tender age of eight years old. You opened your home to me and treated me as your daughter. In loving me, you taught me honor and respect. You not only guided me, but my children and now my grandchildren.

I love you and I appreciate you. I thank you for the love you give so freely from your heart. I thank God for blessing me to be a part of your life both spiritually and socially.

Each time I look at my certificate on the wall I thank you for encouraging me to accept the scholarship into seminary. I was scared, but you wouldn't allow me to buckle under that fear. Each semester was a challenge, but I pushed forward. When graduation time came, seeing the look of pride on your face meant so much to me. You knew from the beginning that I was able and I would not only succeed but excel in my studies.

You taught me that if I surrender my dreams to God I can take the word "if" out of my vocabulary and replace it with "when."

I never imagined you not being here. It has been a painful journey without you. I'll never forget your words of wisdom and encouragement. I govern my life by a statement you made when I first told you how much I love to write poetry. You told me, "Beulah, God doesn't accept junk. Whatever you do for Him, must be done decently and in order." I pray my life will forever display the prayers you prayed for me and the transparent life you lived before me. I love you.

Titus 2:3-5

BOTCHED BUT BEAUTIFUL

My Friend: Cathy Ozan

Before I began this dedication of friendship I wanted a greater understanding of what a true friend is, because Exodus 33:11 says, "God spoke to Moses as one speaks with a friend," and James 2:23 says, "Abraham was called a friend of God."

Before I go further I would like to share a couple of definitions I found for friend:

1. A person whom one knows, likes, and trust.
2. One who supports, strengthens, and sympathizes with.

I never would have imagined a bond of friendship could grow in such depth and loyalty from my daughter asking you to hold your daughter, when they were both babies. I'll always remember the smile you gave Verna as you placed Sherita on her lap. You never let her know you still had a hold of your baby while allowing her to feel like a big girl. We serve an awesome God that knew it would take the simple, but compound love of our children to bring us together as friends.

Through the years we haven't hung out much
or called each other every day, but our
friendship continues to grow and strengthen.
You became a spiritual anchor in my life.
Your faith in God is strong and sturdy,
unshakable and without doubt or fear. You
show me by the life you live how to stand,
unmovable, on the Word of God.

As our children faced many obstacles through
the years, I can't remember you ever telling
me to calm down. You always showed me how
to relax and have confidence in God.

Early on I saw spiritual strength radiating in
your life. You never accepted defeat, but most
of all you never compromised your true
identity. As my peer, and friend, your life
spoke louder than you'll ever know. Your
word has always been like a spoken contract.
If Cathy said it, then Cathy did it. You live a
life of truth and transparency that still amazes
me to this day.

Your encouragement, support, and prayers
will forever be appreciated. You never allowed
me to give up on the gift God has given me.
My greatest advice from you came in the midst
of one of our casual conversations. You told

me, "In God's time he's going to open doors no man can shut." I smiled and nodded. You told me, "Beulah, God has your season already set. He has to get you ready for what he has for you. Stay focused and be prepared because when it comes you're going to blow up girl!" We laughed and our conversation once again changed to our children.

As God moves me into my journey I constantly reflect on your words of wisdom. I surround myself with your friendship even when we are miles apart. As you go through your day know that you have a friend that is lifting you before the Father. I pray the anchor and friend you have been to me, I pass it on to others. I love you.

Proverbs 18:24

My Sisters: Lolita Woods, Myranda Davis

Before I needed friends, I knew I had sisters,

My strength, my confidants, my greatest listeners.

We told each other of our lives dreams.

We leaned on each other and became a solid team.

When life was hard and happiness amiss,

We became a force to be reckoned with.

If you touched one, you had to face the others.

If you got past us, you'd have to face our brothers.

Bonded tightly like a three string cord, we stuck together

Through thick and thin.

Our mother woven through us; her character and faith

Made us a tenacious blend.

Life and age may separate us physically,

But our hearts claim us as sisters for life.

"For I know the plans I have for you," declares the LORD, "plans to prosper you and not to harm you, plans to give you hope and a future."

Jeremiah 29:11

The thief cometh not, but for to steal,
and to kill, and to destroy: I am come
that they might have life, and that
they might have it more abundantly.

John 10:10

Our greatest weapons for healing are:
Faith in God and the ability to believe,
all things work together for good to
them that love God, to them who are
the called according to his purpose.

This portion of poetry is dedicated to

my will to live and not die.

Flashback

Sometimes my mind flashes back to a time when I didn't understand.

I would hear my mama singing, asking God to please take her hand.

Where would He take her? Would us kids be able to go?

Would He take her away from him, so he wouldn't hit her anymore?

Would God take us to a place where we could see her smile?

Would there be peace, if only for a while?

Sometimes I flashback to when I used to pray.

"God my mama is so beautiful and she is very nice.

She helps everyone around us, so why don't he treat her right?"

Many nights we were afraid, even scared to go to sleep.

We were threatened to not make a sound,

So we would lay there without a peep.

Then there was the night that I heard mama screaming.

"Oh God," I thought, "Please let me be dreaming."

But, I wasn't! So, I crouched down in the corner.

Then I heard it, click, click, boom!

I heard it again, click, click, boom!

The noise it was so loud. Was it coming for me?

I didn't want to take that chance.

 I was frozen still. I could not move.

Oh no, I think I wet my pants.

I stayed there in the corner that was now my safety place.

I watched my mama sit there with a blank look on her face.

I could now hear her crying. "What's the matter?" I wanted to ask, "Is someone dying?"

BOTCHED BUT BEAUTIFUL

As my mind flashes back, I remember the sirens

And all of the lights. Police were everywhere.

"Is my mama all right?" I remember asking.

I heard someone answer, "Yes, she is over there."

At first, I thought God had finally taken her hand

And He was leading her on.

Then I realized, I'm still here, so I knew she wasn't gone.

God kept us safe and He kept mama strong.

By the next day we were all back at home.

So now when I think of God's protection and provision,

It doesn't take a lot to get me back on track.

I only have to sit a moment and have a flashback.

Damn You!

Damn you! Yes, that's what I said.

You heard exactly what you thought you
heard.

I lived in a silent hell that you created for me,

Not being able to talk, not able to say a word.

Your hell had me strangled, it had me
confused,

It had me feeling abandoned and bruised.

Damn You! For making me suffer so long.

You stole my innocence, you tarnished my joy.

You knew what you were doing, you also knew
it was wrong.

You read the book I wrote? You're shocked
that I remember.

The nightmares that followed, you're the one I
blame.

Oh, pick your head up, I want you to feel some
of this shame.

BOTCHED BUT BEAUTIFUL

Damn you! For making me keep this hell
buried inside, because

I couldn't handle the hurt or the pain you
made me feel.

Then I realized after all these years, if I
continued to keep it hidden

I would never be able to heal.

One night at my lowest; Like this I knew I
couldn't go on.

I cried out to my Savior, "Please Father, take
all of this away.

Please let it be gone.

I'm tired. I'm ready to let it go. I'm ready to
move on."

GOD helped me, He freed me, He took the
emptiness away.

Then He held me, He rocked me, and put
peace in its place.

That is the night I learned true forgiveness.

Yes, that is the night He restored my joy to live
again.

Since thin I have been doing all that He has
assigned for me to do.

I surrendered, I forgave, I even withdrew the
statement I made,

Damn You!

Demons Creep

My nights are filled with sweat and tears.

I thought I had gotten rid of all my childhood fears.

Demons I had hidden for so long,

Buried so deep, I thought they were gone.

With one conversation they all came back,

And not trying to cut me any slack.

I'm tossing and turning, trying to sleep.

I feel vulnerable and lost like straying sheep.

I'm still trying to stay in control of emotions running wild,

But I'm feeling helpless as a child.

"Not again," to the Lord I pray.

"Not the feelings of low self esteem

This alone will kill all of my dreams."

Each day I've been struggling to run the voices
out of my head.

I hear them very clearly, by now they thought
I'd be dead.

Once again I'm fighting through guilt and
shame.

But this time I'm facing those demons,

I refuse to further cast any blame.

God has forgiven me and cleansed me from
within.

I decree to the demons, "You shall not win.

I am covered with the blood of Jesus and now
I'm born again."

My tears are flowing free, I choose to rejoice.

Through fasting and praying, I now hear The
Master's voice.

BOTCHED BUT BEAUTIFUL

Now, I must warn you, beware of the demons you did not face.

If you do not handle them, they will only sleep.

They will wait for years, but let me assure you, demons do creep.

Gone So Soon

Oh Lord, my Father, please take this pain away.

I wanted this to be a brighter day.

I sit in my room alone once again

Crying, but wanting to scream

From the battle locked within.

Bomb, I'm sorry for the demons you had to fight alone.

I didn't understand them all until you were gone.

I would have stood by you

And we could have both taken a stand

Against the hurt, betrayal, and shame,

Caused by the selfishness of someone else's hand.

I could have, I would have

Showed you life was still worth living.

BOTCHED BUT BEAUTIFUL

You didn't have to keep being locked away

Afraid to accept the love we were giving.

I will never forget the knock on my door.

It was 9:13 on Thursday, August 19th.

That day I stood by your bed side

Promising to be strong,

Trying to sift through everything,

To see where life went wrong.

I watched the machines

As they made your chest rise and fall.

I'm seeing it, but still not comprehending it all.

I leaned over to tell you again,

"BZ is here, and it's ok to give up the fight,

For you have been fighting all of your life."

I guess you heard my voice

For the rise and fall of your chest

Seemed to have gotten slower.

I knew it wouldn't be long before you would be gone.

At 11:42pm you took your last breath

And then you went on home.

The exact time is a time I'll never mourn,

For that is exactly the time your niece Rusty was born.

Today my heart is engulfed in sorrow.

Because I promised to be strong,

I know it will be better tomorrow.

Right now I wish you could talk to me.

So I could hear you say,

"I love you sis, you will always be my BZ,

Don't ever let that fade away."

BOTCHED BUT BEAUTIFUL

I know you got everything right with God and

You are in that heavenly place.

I still have things that I am assigned to do,

But rest assured my time will come

When I will finish my race.

What a day that will be

When we meet again face to face.

(Dedicated to my brother Herman Hall Jr.)

He was known to family and friends as Bomb.

Resting in Him

Close your eyes and feel me as I fill you.

Know My voice, know My touch,

Know that I love you very much.

Shh, don't say anything,

Just enjoy My tender embrace,

Feel the softness as I caress your face.

Now, lay your head in My bosom, relax and go
to sleep.

Do not worry, I have you covered.

I am the Shepherd and you are My sheep.

Let me hold you closer as I wrap you in My
arms.

I know you have never felt this safe,

But, there is no need to be alarmed

BOTCHED BUT BEAUTIFUL

My Father sent Me to watch over you,

Because you have accepted Me by faith.

You are now filled with Our spirit

And covered by mercy and grace.

Dying To Drink

I'm facing reality, my brother is going to die,

This time I don't have to ask or even wonder why.

It's hard to stand by, doing my best to fight,

Trying to get him to see, that, the alcohol is destroying his life.

My heart hurts each time I see him take a drink.

I ask him to stop, take a moment, and think.

His steps are not only getting slower, they are filled with pain,

Leading him down a road with nothing to gain.

Life may not be great, or even that grand,

But he's killing himself with each sip he takes

From that damn beer can.

I try to explain, his body is not made for that liquid beating

BOTCHED BUT BEAUTIFUL

And all the pain he is feeling, is from his liver's pleadings.

The options are plenty, the drink of choice

Used to block and shut out that unwelcomed voice.

Pay attention, when one drink becomes two, three, or maybe four,

When you can't stand up straight or walk to the door.

Its grip is subtle and may even take years

For you to realize that you have graduated from the beers.

Alcohol grips you like it's holding a grudge,

Declaring itself to be the stronger drug.

It is a drug, not covered under the law,

By the death of so many, it takes a bow.

I heard it is called "rot gut" from the damage it does.

You won't understand until it grips someone you love.

My message today, I hope is clear,

Push the drinks aside, and keep those you love near.

Please listen to this message that I deploy.

Alcohol is a demon meant to destroy!

Mirrors

I declared my body is my temple, undefiled and untouched.

 Yet, underneath it all, I didn't like it very much.

The full length mirror was my enemy, in front of it I could not stand.

I would cry and become depressed as I failed another diet plan.

Most of my life I struggled with being called fat or over weight.

Don't people realize how much their words hurt?

BOTCHED BUT BEAUTIFUL

I came to the realization that I am fearfully
and wonderfully made.

In God's eyes I am very appealing,

For He molded me perfectly on His potter's
wheel.

Now, when I look in the mirror,

I see a queen staring back at me.

I'm not vain or full of myself,

But if I don't believe it,

Neither will anyone else.

My royalty has been bought with a price.

There were aches, pain, and sorrow,

But the cost was worth saving my life.

I am a daughter of God the Father

My beauty radiates from within.

It is not determined by

My size or the color of my skin.

The mirror is now my friend,

It reflects my true identity.

I am a woman of love, laughter,

Peace, and calm serenity.

Today I shout out in a melodious tune.

 As its volume fills the room, the message is clear and true.

I am beautiful, I am phenomenal, I am Beulah Neveu.

BOTCHED BUT BEAUTIFUL

Reclaiming Royalty

We've given to much power to hands that were unclean, disloyal, ugly, unstable, and hearts that were mean.

We were duped, tricked, by wolves in sheep's clothes.

We were treated with tenderness, our hearts taught to disrobe.

We learned to laugh, when we really wanted to cry.

Keeping emotions in check, making smiling a mental task.

We're getting tired, but we want to live

And strip off your oppressive mask.

We became trapped, paying too much for what was supposed to be free.

Now from a prison without bars, on a quest for liberty

We must search within ourselves for a sense of tranquility.

We must cover our bodies, respect who we
are, wives, daughters, mothers, and so much
more.

We have many titles that we must bare, but

Being a child of God is our greatest honor for
sure.

The Bible says, "Our worth is far above
rubies."

So, we must demand to be treated like the
queens that we are.

Increasing our faith, building our character,

Raising our standards to a higher bar.

We must embrace who we are.

Enjoy being the women we were created to be,

Determined, with purpose, strength, and
dignity.

Stand up Royal queen,

Beautiful woman, we are stronger than we
know.

We must search inside ourselves, know our
worth, and then let it show.

Glory From My Story

Life is a story, yet its time is fleeing,

Filled with fighting, screaming, whippings, and beatings.

Dreams became nightmares that were traumatic,

Feelings unstable, emotions erratic.

Seeing more and wanting more,

Trying to break through solid doors.

Life was still moving, time flying by,

No time to stop to wonder why,

I kept being broken, battered, and bruised,

Taken for granted, shattered, and misused.

I decided I had had enough.

I wasn't taking any more of Satan's stuff.

I stood my ground, I stood firm,

I grabbed a hold of the Father's arm.

He took my feet and planted them solid as a rock.

It was then that I learned that my belief can be shaken,

But my faith cannot.

Now, I can see God's hand was moving in my story.

 Life has been rough, but it has all been

For my good and His glory.

So many scars, more than I was due.

But today I rejoice, I thank the LORD that I don't look like

All the hell that I've been through.

Botched But Beautiful

My heart hold stories that's never been told,

Things that tried to kill me and destroy my soul.

I'd been set up from the beginning to fail,

Molested, beaten, rejected, my innocence derailed.

I've been called ugly, fat, a shameful disgrace,

Always behind my back, never to my face.

I've been lied to, cheated on, nose turned up in scrutiny,

Therefore, trust and security were words that were foreign to me.

I have scars that are hidden from the naked eyes,

Safely guarded and stashed inside.

Mishandled, my life was made a mess,

BOTCHED, was the title given to me

For flunking life's first big test.

But, life was mistaken. I wouldn't allow that
to be my final grade,

As I began to realize I'm perfectly and
wonderfully made.

The more God blessed me with days to live

I started drawing from the strength I watched
my mama give.

I learned it was okay to cry,

As long as I don't drown in my tears and lay
down to die.

Weeping really does endure for a night,

God promises me everything will be alright.

Now, I can laugh from the inside out,

Because I'm learning what walking a godly life
is really all about.

I am BEAUTIFUL, a pleasure to behold, God
has cancelled out the old.

I now have new stories that need to be told.

Stories that flow from within my heart,

BOTCHED BUT BEAUTIFUL

Saying I'm strong, I'm wise, I'm holy, and I'm smart.

I'm not vain by the use of so many I's.

I is who I am, I'm on eagle's wings ready to fly.

The past is my runway, the present my plane,

The future full of possibilities that God has lain.

To deny my past is to deny who I've become,

A virtuous woman whose life has been touched by the Holy One.

What the enemy meant for bad, God already knew it would be for my good.

I stand boldly today, Botched But Beautiful.

About the Author

Beulah Hall Neveu is a native Houstonian. She attended school in the Houston ISD. Beulah received her certification in Women's Ministry at South Western Baptist Theological Seminary in Houston, TX. She is an active member of Greater Saint Matthew Church where she serves on The Women's Power Team and teaches Monday night Bible class.

Beulah began writing poetry at the age of sixteen. It was her love for poetry that inspired her love for reading. She is now enjoying her new love, writing. Beulah loves playing jacks, writing, reading, and music of all genres.